SPORTS'
TOP
MVPS™

LEBRON JAMES

SIMONE PAYMENT

rosen publishing's
rosen
central®

New York

Published in 2019 by The Rosen Publishing Group, Inc.
29 East 21st Street, New York, NY 10010

First Edition

Library of Congress Cataloging-in-Publication Data

Names: Payment, Simone, author.
Title: LeBron James / Simone Payment.
Description: New York : Rosen Central, 2019. | Series: Sports' Top MVPs
| Includes bibliographical references and index. | Audience: Grades: 5–8.
Identifiers: LCCN 2017050385| ISBN 9781508182078 (library bound) |
ISBN 9781508182085 (paperback)
Subjects: LCSH: James, LeBron—Juvenile literature. | Basketball play-
ers—United States—Juvenile literature. | African American basketball
players—Biography—Juvenile literature.
Classification: LCC GV884.J36 P39 2019 | DDC 796.323092 [B]
—dc23
LC record available at https://lccn.loc.gov/2017050385

Manufactured in the United States of America

On the cover: LeBron James dunks in the third quarter against
the Boston Celtics during Game Five of the 2017 NBA Eastern
Conference Finals.

CONTENTS

Life wasn't always easy for LeBron James when he was growing up in Akron, Ohio. He never knew his father. His mother was very young when LeBron was born. He and his mom moved a lot when he was young. They did not have a lot of money for clothes or sneakers or even for food.

When LeBron was in fourth grade, he began to discover that he had a talent for sports. He was good at football and dreamed of becoming a professional football player, but it turned out that LeBron was also very good at basketball. It was basketball that would make his dreams of playing a professional sport come true. LeBron grew up to become one of the most talented basketball players ever to play the sport. Sports fans and teammates all agree he is a superstar.

LeBron's basketball talent stood out even in junior high school. In high school, he and his teammates won the Ohio state championship three out of four years. People around the country were taking notice of how talented he was. At seventeen, he appeared on the cover of *Sports Illustrated* magazine. As soon as he finished high school, the Cleveland Cavaliers drafted him.

James quickly became a top National Basketball Association (NBA) player. The Cavaliers did not have a good team when he arrived. They slowly improved year after year and began going to the NBA playoffs. However, without winning a championship, James decided to leave Cleveland. He joined the Miami Heat, and there he won two NBA championships. James kept thinking about Cleveland, though. He wanted to bring an NBA championship to his hometown. In 2015, he returned to the Cleveland Cavaliers and the next year they won the NBA championship.

Tied with a minute to go in Game 7 of the 2016 NBA Finals, James and the Cleveland Cavaliers pulled through and won Cleveland's first NBA championship.

LeBron James is a powerful player. He scores many points each game. He often has many steals and assists as well. James is also known as a very smart basketball player. He looks ahead to what other players may do. As good as James already is, he is always trying to improve his basketball playing.

He also tries to make life better for other people. With his LeBron James Family Foundation he helps young people in his community. He also mentors young players about basketball and about life. When asked about his goals in 2017, he told an interviewer, "My next goal is to continue to get better and better. [I want to] work hard and strive for greatness every day."

CHAPTER ONE

A FUTURE STAR

LeBron Raymone James was born in Akron, Ohio, on December 30, 1984. His mother, Gloria, was sixteen years old, so Gloria and LeBron lived with Gloria's mother. Gloria's older brother Terry and younger brother Curt also lived with them. LeBron's father has never been involved in LeBron's life.

When LeBron was eight months old, Gloria met Eddie Jackson and they began dating. Ever since, Eddie Jackson has been like a father to LeBron. Jackson loved playing with LeBron. Just before LeBron turned three, Gloria and Jackson got him a child-size basketball hoop for Christmas. LeBron loved it, and played with it often.

That same Christmas, things changed for James and his family. On Christmas Eve, his grandmother had a heart attack. She died a few days later. Gloria was nineteen, Terry was twenty-two, and Curt was just twelve. They were not able to pay for their house, so they were forced to move. They all went to different places. Gloria and LeBron lived for a while with some neighbors, the Reaves family. They had a wooden box nailed to a pole in the yard. LeBron used this as a basketball hoop.

After they lived with the Reaves family, Gloria and LeBron moved from place to place, staying with friends. When LeBron was five years old, he and Gloria moved seven times. Eventually, they moved to a housing project called Elizabeth Park. There was a lot of crime in the neighborhood, and the houses were not in good shape. Looking back on it now that he is an adult, LeBron talked to *Sports Illustrated* about Elizabeth Park. "It was a mess. … There was violence. I saw so much I wouldn't want my kids to see."

BEFORE BASKETBALL THERE WAS FOOTBALL

LeBron's first sport was football. When he was nine years old, LeBron joined a football team and loved it. He decided he would one day play in the National Football League. He liked playing with other kids who had similar interests. He also liked the structure that the rules provided to the game.

The coach of LeBron's team was Frankie Walker. Coach Walker could see that LeBron was a talented athlete. He could also see that LeBron's life outside football was not easy. LeBron and his mom were still moving often. In fourth grade, LeBron missed eighty-seven days of school. Coach Walker thought it would be a good idea for LeBron to come live with him and his family. Coach Walker's wife, Pam, and their three kids welcomed LeBron.

As a member of the Northeast Shooting Stars, LeBron stood out. He and his teammates eventually played in the national AAU championship game in 1999, losing the game by just two points.

He lived with them during the week and then spent the weekends with his mom.

At the Walkers' house, LeBron had to do chores and there were rules about things like when to go to bed. He also had to make sure his homework was always done. Still, LeBron had a lot of fun living with the Walkers. There was a basketball hoop in the driveway, and LeBron played often. Frankie Walker also coached basketball teams and he noticed that LeBron was very good at that sport, too. LeBron carefully studied the rules of basketball and the techniques other players used. He wanted to learn as much as possible about the game.

After fifth grade, LeBron returned to live with his mother full time. She had an apartment. She also kept up with the rules LeBron had learned at the Walker house. One rule was that schoolwork had to come first.

A BASKETBALL PLAYER AND COACH

While he was still living with the Walkers, LeBron joined the basketball team Frankie Walker coached. He spent much of his free time practicing. The second year LeBron was on the team, Frankie Walker asked LeBron to help him coach the fourth-grade team. LeBron was only in fifth grade himself, but he was an excellent teacher to the younger kids.

That same year, LeBron joined an Amateur Athletic Union (AAU) basketball team. The team name was the Northeast Shooting Stars. Dru Joyce II was the coach and his son, Dru Joyce III, was also on the team. He was known as Little Dru, and he and LeBron became good friends. LeBron also became close friends with two other boys on the team, named Sian Cotton and Willie McGee. The four boys played together all through junior high school on the Shooting Stars. They became known as the Fabulous Four or the Fab Four.

The Shooting Stars traveled around Ohio playing teams from other towns. Playing on this travel team, LeBron got to know other top players in Ohio. He continued to practice and develop his basketball skills.

HIGH SCHOOL SUPERSTAR

Near the end of his time in junior high school, LeBron had to decide where to go to high school. He and Dru Joyce III, Sian Cotton, and Willie McGee all decided to go to St. Vincent–St. Mary (SVSM) High School. SVSM is a small Catholic high school in Akron. It is known for its emphasis on schoolwork. SVSM was also known for its excellent basketball coach, Keith Dambrot. The Fab Four knew they would have to work hard in their studies at SVSM, but they also wanted to win the Ohio state basketball championship. They believed Dambrot could help them do that.

LeBron plays a game during his senior year in Greensboro, North Carolina.

In his freshman year at SVSM, LeBron played on the football team. He started as a wide receiver on the junior varsity team. He was so good that partway through the season, he was moved up to the varsity team. When the basketball season started, most of LeBron's attention was on the basketball court. He also had to focus on his schoolwork. In order to play on sports teams, SVSM required students to get good grades.

Just as the Fab Four had hoped, in their first year at SVSM, they had a terrific basketball team. LeBron played point guard. He and his teammates

During LeBron's first two years at SVSM, his coach was Keith Dambrot. Dambrot went on to coach college teams, including thirteen seasons at the University of Akron, where his record was 305 wins and 139 losses.

won the Ohio state basketball championship. LeBron scored twenty-five points in the championship game.

Over the summer after his freshman year, LeBron played in basketball camps around the country. LeBron also grew three inches (eight centimeters) that summer. He was now six feet seven inches (two meters). When the fall came, he played on the football team again.

That year, there was a new addition to the basketball team, Romeo Travis. With Romeo on the team, they became the "Fabulous Five." The team lost only one game all year. The game they lost, they lost only by one point. Again, they went to the Ohio state basketball championship. Again, they won. LeBron won the Most Valuable Player (MVP) Award for the Ohio Division III State Championship. He also was on the All-State team. In addition, he won the Mr. Basketball award, as the best high school player in Ohio.

SPORTS ILLUSTRATED COVER BOY

Many people in Ohio knew who LeBron was. People around the country who followed high school basketball might have known him, too. Anyone in the United States interested in sports, however, was introduced to LeBron on February 18, 2002. That day, LeBron appeared on the cover of *Sports Illustrated* magazine. He was now a seventeen-year-old basketball superstar.

** *Sports Illustrated* compared him to Michael Jordan. At the time, Jordan was a top NBA player. They also said he was better than other NBA stars had been when they were in high school. They correctly predicted that he would become an NBA superstar himself.**

Basketball fans in other parts of the country were starting to hear about LeBron. He was added to *USA Today's* All-America high school basketball team. The team was made up of top players from around the country.

In his junior year at SVSM, LeBron played football again. The team went to the state semifinals. During the playoffs, however, LeBron broke his left index finger. That made him decide it would be his last year of football. LeBron's finger healed in time for the basketball season.

Through the season, the team did well, just not as well as in previous years. For the first time, they lost the state championship. Even though the team did not do as well, LeBron had an amazing season. For the second time, he won the Mr. Basketball award. He was also named the Gatorade National Boys Basketball Player of the Year. It was during this year that people around Ohio began calling him King James.

UNDER THE MICROSCOPE

There was a lot of attention on LeBron for his athletic talent. Officials were also watching him closely to make sure he wasn't breaking any rules. In January 2003, Ohio sports officials investigated a report that LeBron was driving an expensive Hummer SUV. It had leather seats and televisions in it. Some thought it might have been a gift from a company that wanted LeBron to do advertising for them. This is against the rules for high school players. It turned out that LeBron's mother had taken out a loan to buy it for him. LeBron also got in trouble for accepting two expensive football jerseys from a store in Cleveland. As a punishment, LeBron had to miss two games and SVSM had to forfeit one game.

PREPARING FOR THE NEXT STEP

After his junior year, many colleges tried to get LeBron to come play for their team. He was more interested in going directly to playing for an NBA team. LeBron was even interested in skipping his senior year of high school and starting his professional basketball career, but the NBA had a rule that only high school graduates could join the league. LeBron asked the NBA to change the rules, but they would not.

Over the summer, LeBron broke his wrist playing in a summer league game. He missed much of the summer but was still able to go to some basketball camps.

When the basketball season started, LeBron was ready to play. There was a lot of pressure for him to play well. After the *Sports Illustrated* cover, there were many articles and TV reports about

LeBron. There was so much interest in him that national television channel ESPN2 decided to broadcast one of his high school games. This was the first time a high school game had appeared on national television. LeBron was not the only future NBA star who played in that game. Carmelo Anthony played for the other team. LeBron and SVSM were the winners of the game, 65–45. LeBron scored 31 of those points himself.

By the end of LeBron's senior year, the SVSM basketball team had won twenty-four games. They lost only one game—the game they had had to forfeit. That meant they won every game they played that year. They won the state championship for the third time in four years. LeBron was also named Mr. Basketball again. After the season, SVSM retired LeBron's jersey with its #23. In his high school career, LeBron had scored 2,657 points and had 892 rebounds and 523 assists.

Luol Deng and Chris Paul were LeBron's teammates on the McDonald's High School All-American team.

At the end of the basketball season, LeBron played in the McDonald's High School All-American game. Top high school players competed in the game. With LeBron's help, his team won, 122–107. LeBron won the John Wooden Award as MVP of the team.

CHAPTER TWO

FROM "SHOOTING STAR" TO NBA SUPERSTAR

With high school behind him, LeBron James looked ahead to the NBA. His professional basketball career started when he was drafted on June 6, 2003. The Cleveland Cavaliers had the first pick of the draft that year. They chose James. James's hometown of Akron is less than forty miles (sixty-four kilometers) from Cleveland. So it was almost as if the Cavaliers were his hometown team. James had long dreamed of being in the NBA. He still considers being drafted a high point of his career. He told interviewer Mallory Chin in 2017 that "as you put your mind to things and you think about things, they become true. [My] dream came true for an 18-year-old kid coming out of Akron, Ohio, to be … a part of the NBA."

James had a busy summer. He did a lot of interviews with newspapers, magazines, and sports TV channels. He went to Los Angeles with some friends. He also did business deals. His biggest deal was signing with Nike for $90 million. In addition, he signed a deal with Upper Deck, a sports and entertainment company, for $5 million. This was in addition to the $11 million the Cavaliers would pay him over three years.

NBA ROOKIE

For James's first game with the Cavaliers, twenty thousand people showed up to watch. The Cavaliers had not been a very good team. People hoped James could help change that. In his first game, he certainly tried. James scored twenty-five points, had six rebounds, nine assists, and four steals. The Cavaliers lost the game anyway.

Over James's first season, he played as well as NBA players who had been in the league for years. Many of them were much older. During the season, he scored an average of 20.9 points per game. James won the NBA Rookie of the Year award. He was the youngest winner of that award in NBA history. He was also the first Cleveland Cavalier to ever win that award.

In 2003, James was featured on the cover of *SportingNews*, alongside Carmelo Anthony.

Although the Cavaliers ended the season with a losing record, fans had hope. They believed James could eventually turn things around for the team.

During the offseason, something happened that changed the way James thought about basketball. On October 4, 2004, LeBron had a son with his girlfriend, Savannah Brinson. He and Brinson had met in high school. They named the baby LeBron James Jr. The birth of his son made LeBron realize there was more to life than basketball. It helped him get over losing games more quickly. Having a child also made him appreciate his mother even more. As a single mom, she had been both mother and father to LeBron. She had given up a lot to raise him on her own.

LEBRON JAMES FAMILY FOUNDATION

In 2004, LeBron started the LeBron James Family Foundation. This charity organization focuses on helping kids in Cleveland and Akron, as well as across the United States. In honor of LeBron's mom, they try to help kids of single parents in particular.

The foundation raises money for the YMCA and other local groups. They also work with Boys Hope Girls Hope. This group helps get kids into temporary homes if their families are facing difficulties.

In 2011, James's foundation started the I Promise program to help keep kids in school. James mentors the young people in the program, writing them weekly letters. He hosts them at games and events and helps buy school supplies and uniforms. James won the 2006 NBA Community Assist Award for his work with the LeBron James Family Foundation. He also won the 2017 J. Walter Kennedy Citizenship Award from the Professional Basketball Writers Association. This honor was for all the work he has done in his community.

BUILDING A TEAM

During James's second season on the team, the Cavaliers steadily improved. The 2004–2005 Cavaliers had a winning record of 42–40. It was the first time in seven years that the Cavaliers had won more games than they lost.

James played on his first NBA All-Star team that year, scoring thirteen points. He finished the season with the third-highest points total of any player in the NBA that season. In one game, he scored fifty-six points. He was the youngest player to ever score that many points in a game.

In James's second season with the Cavaliers, he continued to break records. On November 13, 2005, James hit four thousand points. He was the youngest player ever to hit that mark. James also went to his second NBA All-Star game and his team won. James scored twenty-nine points during the game and won the MVP award. He was the youngest player ever to win the All-Star Game MVP award.

The 2005–2006 season was a success for the Cavaliers. The team went to the NBA playoffs for the first time in eight years. In the first round of the playoffs, they beat the Washington Wizards in six games. In the second round, they fought hard but lost to the Detroit Pistons in seven games. After the season, the Cavaliers gave James a three-year contract extension.

While playing on the Rookies team at the 2004 All-Star Rookie Challenge game, James dunked against the Sophomore team.

GETTING CLOSER TO A CHAMPIONSHIP

Over the next few years, the Cavaliers continued to improve their record. In the 2006–2007 season, their record was fifty wins and thirty-two losses, and they went all the way to the NBA Finals, where they were swept by the San Antonio Spurs. In the 2007–2008 season, they went to the second round of the NBA playoffs. The Cavaliers lost the seventh game, 97–92, to the Boston Celtics. During the 2008–2009 season, the Cavaliers won an impressive sixty-six games. It seemed like

At the 2008 NBA All-Star game, James won the MVP Award playing on the East team.

the Cavaliers might finally be on track to win the NBA championship. This seemed even more possible when they swept the first two rounds of the playoffs. They beat the Detroit Pistons in the first round and the Atlanta Hawks in the second, but the Cavaliers were not able to beat the Orlando Magic. They were able to win only one game in the Finals.

Throughout those three seasons, James continued his winning ways. He played in the NBA All-Star Game all three years. In the 2007 All-Star Game, he scored twenty-eight points in just thirty-two minutes. In the 2008 All-Star Game, he was named MVP. He also racked up plenty of other amazing statistics. From November 14 through November 27, 2007, he scored thirty or more points in every single game he played. Later in that season, he became the all-time highest scorer for the Cavaliers. In the 2007–2008 season, he reached ten thousand points. He was the youngest-ever NBA player to reach that total. He also scored the most points of anyone in the NBA during that season.

The 2008–2009 season was James's best yet. He won NBA Player of the Month four times. At the end of the season, he had the most points, rebounds, assists, steals, and blocks of anyone on the Cavaliers. He was also named NBA MVP. He was the youngest player ever to win that award. He was twenty-four years old at the time.

During this time, other exciting things were happening in LeBron's life off the basketball court. On June 14, 2007, LeBron's girlfriend had their second son. They named him Bryce Maximus James. In 2009, LeBron wrote a book called *Shooting Stars*. He had help writing the book from Buzz Bissinger. There was also a documentary film made about LeBron's career called *More Than a Game*.

ONE MORE TRY

In the 2009–2010 season, Shaquille O'Neal joined the Cavaliers. Fans thought this might help get the Cavaliers a championship. James continued

By the end of the 2009 season, James was growing frustrated in Cleveland. He played hard every game, but he couldn't win championship games on his own.

scoring points. By March, he had fifteen thousand career points. Once again, he was the youngest player to hit that mark. He also went to the All-Star Game for the sixth time and helped his team win. James was named NBA MVP for the second year in a row.

The Cavaliers won sixty-one of their games that season and played the Chicago Bulls in the first round of the playoffs. By the second round, however, the Cavaliers were out of the playoffs. They lost in six games. Another year, another loss in the playoffs. James was upset and frustrated that the Cavaliers had not yet won an NBA championship. He would soon have a decision to make.

CHAPTER THREE

THE DECISION

At the disappointing end to the 2009–2010 season, James's contract was up with the Cavaliers. He could decide to stay and get a new contract with his hometown team. Or he could join a new team. James met with the Bulls, Clippers, Heat, Knicks, and Nets. All tried to convince him to join their team.

On July 7, 2010, ESPN announced that they would be having a television special called "The Decision." On the program, James would reveal which team he would be joining. The show was broadcast live from the Boys and Girls Club in Greenwich, Connecticut. ESPN announced that they would give the $2.5 million from ads on the show to the Boys and Girls Club.

On the show, James announced, "This fall I'm going to take my talents to South Beach [Florida] and join the Miami Heat. … I want to be able to win championships. And I feel like I can compete down there."

Fans in Cleveland were crushed. The Cavaliers' owners were also upset. They promised fans they would get new players and win a championship without James. James said that he was frustrated that he had not won a championship in Cleveland. He said the team had not had enough top players. Fans were upset anyway. Many were mad that James had planned an hour-long national television show to announce his decision. James didn't look back. He was on his way to Miami.

While being interviewed by Jim Gray, James announced he was leaving for Miami. It was the most-watched television program in Cleveland that night, and Cavaliers fans were very disappointed by James's decision.

BUILDING A NEW TEAM

The day after "The Decision," James went to Miami. The Heat had a party for him and his new teammates. That summer, LeBron moved his family to a waterfront mansion in Miami. Over the summer, LeBron worked out with his new teammates to get ready to start the basketball season.

The Heat's season got off to a slow start. They lost the first game of the 2010–2011 season. Over the first few months, they lost almost as many games as they won. At James's first game back in Cleveland, he was booed by fans nonstop. In that game, however, LeBron scored twenty-four points just in the third quarter. By the end of the game, he had scored 38 points and the Heat won, 118–90. As usual, James played in the All-Star Game that year.

James and his teammates (Dexter Pittman, Mario Chalmers, and Udonis Haslem, from left to right) thought they were ready for the NBA Finals in 2011 but did not win the championship.

By the end of the season, the Heat had won fifty-eight games. That was good enough to go to the playoffs. They won the first, second, and third rounds in five games each. In the Finals, they faced the Dallas Mavericks. James did not play well in the Finals, and the Heat won only two games. Again James was close to his goal of winning an NBA championship, but not close enough.

CHAMPIONS!

In the off-season, James returned to Cleveland to spend the summer there. In September 2011, the Boys and Girls Club of America gave him the Champion of Youth Award. This was for all the work he had done and the money he had raised for children.

During the 2011–2012 NBA season, James hit twenty thousand points and five thousand assists. Again, James was the youngest player ever to hit those marks. James also won the NBA MVP title.

At the end of the regular season, the Heat prepared to once again go to the playoffs. They won the first round in five games and the second round in six games. In the third round, they faced the Celtics. It took them seven games, but they beat them also. In the Finals, the Heat faced the Oklahoma City Thunder. It took the team just five games to beat the Thunder. Finally, LeBron James had won an NBA championship! James made such an important contribution to the series that he was named NBA Finals MVP. After the win, LeBron told the media, "It was a journey. … All the ups and downs, everything that came along with it … . I can finally say that I'm a champion, and I did it the right way. I didn't shortcut

LEBRON THE OLYMPIAN

After his first NBA season, James had joined the 2004 US Olympic basketball team at the Summer Olympics in Athens, Greece. At nineteen, he was the youngest on the team. He was also the first Cavalier ever to be selected for the US Olympic basketball team. The US team won the bronze medal, but James did not play much. Four years later, James joined the 2008 US Olympic basketball team. That year, the Summer Olympics were held in Beijing, China. The 2008 team was nicknamed "The Redeem Team" because they hoped to do better than a bronze medal. The Redeem Team did win the gold medal, with plenty of help from James. The summer after he won the NBA championship, James played on the 2012 US Olympic team again. Once again the team won a gold medal.

anything. I put a lot of hard work and dedication in it, and hard work pays off. It's a great moment."

The 2012–2013 season would turn out to be another terrific one for James and the Heat. The team won twenty-seven games in a row between February 2 and March 24. At the end of the season, sportswriters voted on who should be named the MVP. James got every vote but one. The Heat were also headed to the playoffs again. They swept the Milwaukee Bucks in the first round. In the second round, they lost only one game in the series against the Bulls.

In the third round, they had to play all seven games to beat the Indianapolis Pacers. Then it was time to meet the San Antonio Spurs in the Finals. It took them seven games, but the Heat won the NBA championship for the second year in a row. And again, James was named the NBA Finals MVP.

LeBron's wife Savannah runs a mentoring program for young women called Women of Our Future.

CHANGE IS COMING

Before the next season, LeBron married his longtime girlfriend, Savannah Brinson. They held their wedding in San Diego on September 14, 2013. Soon after the wedding, he began preparing for another season with the Heat.

The 2013–2014 season was a great one for James. He set yet another career record in March when he scored sixty-one points in a single game. He had scored twenty-four points by halftime. Instead of slowing down, in the third quarter alone he scored twenty-five more points.

By the end of the season, the Heat had won fifty-four games and were on their way to the playoffs again. They worked their way through the first three rounds of the playoffs. In the Finals, they would come up against the San Antonio Spurs for the second year in a row. This time it was the Spurs' turn to win the championship. The Heat were not able to win three in a row.

After the season, James faced a decision. He had an option in his contract to leave the Heat if he wanted to become a free agent. It was time to think hard about whether to stay in Miami or move on.

CHAPTER FOUR

HOMETOWN HERO

In early July 2014, LeBron James made his decision about where to play next. He announced it in a letter that appeared in *Sports Illustrated*. He was going back to Cleveland. In his letter, James explained that he had left Cleveland to win a championship. He had accomplished his goal in with the Heat. He had enjoyed his time in Miami. It had almost been like college for him—he got to live in a new place and try new things. He had accomplished his goal of winning an NBA championship. He had a new goal now. He wanted to bring an NBA championship win to his hometown.

James knew it would take more hard work to build a championship team in Cleveland. He was willing to do that hard work. James ended his letter with, "I'm ready to accept the challenge. I'm coming home."

KING JAMES RETURNS

James and his new Cavaliers teammates had a few months to get ready for the season. First James held an event for his LeBron James Family Foundation. It was on August 8, and it was his first time at a public event since he had returned to Cleveland. He had fireworks and a singer at the event. He told the crowd, "I love you; I'm back."

At his first game back with the Cavaliers on October 30, 2014, James was all smiles, even though the Cavaliers lost the game to the Knicks.

In September, he arranged a series of workouts for his Cavaliers teammates. They traveled to Miami to work out together and to get to know each other better. On October 22, LeBron and his wife had their third child, a daughter they named Zhuri.

James's first season back with the Cavaliers had some ups and downs. He suffered knee and back injuries. He missed more games than he ever had before, but the Cavaliers still won fifty-three games and made it into the playoffs. They easily beat their opponents in the first, second, and third rounds of the playoffs. In the Finals, the Cavaliers fought hard against the Golden State Warriors. However, they lost the seventh game. They had come so close, but not yet close enough.

FROM THE COURT TO THE SCREEN

Along with his basketball skills, James has some acting skills as well. In 2007, he hosted *Saturday Night Live*. That same year, he cohosted the ESPY Awards with Jimmy Kimmel. In 2015, he had a large role in the movie *Trainwreck*. The movie starred Amy Schumer and Bill Hader. Hader played a sports agent, and James played himself as a client of Hader. James got excellent reviews for his funny and natural performance. Schumer joked that although James already had a good job, if he decided to get a different one, she thought he could become an actor. James is also a television producer with his company SpringHill Entertainment.

THIS IS IT!

James and the Cavaliers had come so close to winning the Finals in 2015 but still fell short of the championship. James wanted the 2015–2016 season to be different. James and the Cavaliers had a solid season. The team had fifty-seven wins. James continued with his usual average of scoring more than twenty-five points in every game. Those statistics were important, but not as important to him as reaching his ultimate goal of winning a championship for Cleveland. In the first two rounds, the Cavaliers swept, first against Detroit and then Atlanta. The third round was a little more challenging, and it took them six games to advance on to the Finals. They would face the Golden State Warriors, the same team they had lost to the previous year.

Early in the final round, things did not go well for the Cavaliers. They lost the first game by fifteen points. The second game was even worse—they lost 110–77. In the third game, James scored thirty-one points and the Cavaliers won. In Game 4, however, they lost again. No team in the NBA had ever been down 3–1 in the Finals and still won the championship.

In Game 5, the Cavaliers started to turn things around. They won, 112–97. Then in Game 6, James led the team to another win. James put in an amazing performance. He not only scored forty-one points, he also had eight rebounds, eleven assists, four steals, and three

After winning Game 7, James fell to his knees, filled with emotion. He was back on his feet in time to hold the 2016 NBA championship trophy with his teammates.

blocks. With the Cavaliers' win in Game 6, the two teams were now tied. Just like the previous year, the Cavaliers and Warriors would be battling for the championship in Game 7. In the final game, James was feeling the pressure. He had won two championships in Miami, but a Cleveland win would mean a lot more. He wanted to do well for his hometown. He wanted to do well for his teammates. He also wanted to do well for himself. James and the Cavaliers did all that and more. They battled all through Game 7 and beat the Warriors, 93–89. James and the Cavaliers were finally NBA champions!

James immediately thought about how long Cleveland had waited for a sports championship. This was Cleveland's first championship win— for any of their professional sports teams—since 1964. He was proud to have played a part in bringing a win to his hometown. LeBron also thought about his family, he told *Sports Illustrated*. He also "thought about … the people who supported me when I didn't have a dime to my name, and my life was a struggle. There were so many emotions—too many to hold onto." For his performance throughout the playoffs, James was voted Finals MVP.

Sports fans in the Cleveland area and all over Ohio celebrated for days. After the final game, James had predicted to the media that the celebration would be "the biggest party Cleveland has ever seen." He may have been right. At the victory parade in Cleveland, 1.3 million fans came out to cheer on the team.

ANOTHER YEAR, ANOTHER BATTLE WITH THE WARRIORS

Some players might think they could relax after a big victory like winning the NBA Finals. James was not one of those players. As he told the media after Game 7, "I want to continue to be great. I want to continue

SPEAKING OUT AGAIN

Earlier in his career, James had spoken out against racism and social injustice. Several incidents happened in 2017 that made him want to continue his activism. In late May, someone spray-painted racist graffiti on his house. James spoke about it at a press conference, saying, "No matter how much money you have, no matter how famous you are, no matter how many people admire you, being black in America is tough. We have got a long way to go as a society and for us as African Americans, until we feel equal in America."

He continued speaking out after President Trump criticized football players who were protesting police treatment of black people. James talked about the power of sports to bring people of all kinds together. He discussed the importance of being a leader, saying at a press conference, "I will lend my voice, I will lend passion, I will lend my money, I will lend my resources to … let kids know that there is hope, … and not one individual, no matter if it's the president of the United States or if it's someone in your household, can stop your dreams from becoming a reality."

to lead … my team. I got to continue to be great. That's it. I owe that to myself."

For the 2016–2017 season, James got right back to work. He was not slowing down at all and had another great season. And once again, at the end of the season, he and his teammates played in the NBA playoffs. They swept the first two rounds, first against Indiana and then against Toronto. It took them five games, but they beat the Boston Celtics in the third round. They were back in the Finals. And again, they would be playing the Warriors.

In 2017, James was the NBA's highest-paid player. James is very careful with his money and also gives a lot of money away through the LeBron James Family Foundation.

In 2017, the Cavaliers could not pull off the win. James had some of his best performances ever in the games against the Warriors, but it was not enough. The Cavaliers lost to the Warriors in five games.

James is very competitive so any loss is a hard one, but he felt he had done everything he could. After Game 5, he was already looking ahead to the next year. He told reporters after the game: "I've always told myself, if you feel like you put in the work and you leave it out on the floor, then you can always push forward and not look backwards." James has always done just that. He has worked hard, pushed ahead, and tried to help others along the way.

FACT SHEET

Full name
LeBron Raymone James
Birth date
December 30, 1984
Hometown
Akron, Ohio
Height
6 feet 8 inches (2 m)
Weight
250 pounds (114 kg)
High school
St. Vincent-St. Mary
NBA teams
Cleveland Cavaliers, Miami Heat
Shoots
Right
Position
Power forward, small forward, shooting guard
Uniform number: 23
Amateur awards
Mr. Basketball award (2000–2001,

2001–2002, 2002–2003), USA Today All-America team (2000–2001), Gatorade National Boys Basketball Player of the Year (2001–2002), John Wooden Award (MVP) of McDonald's High School All-American game (2003)
NBA awards
NBA Rookie of the Year Award (2004), NBA MVP (2009, 2010, 2012, 2013), NBA Finals MVP (2012, 2013, 2016), All-Star Game MVP (2006, 2008), NBA top scorer (2008), J. Walter Kennedy Citizenship Award (2017)
All-Star teams
2005– 2017
Olympic teams
2004 (bronze), 2008 (gold), 2012 (gold)

TIMELINE

1984   LeBron Raymone James is born on December 30, in Akron, Ohio.

1994   LeBron joins an Amateur Athletic Union team.

2002   LeBron appears on the cover of *Sports Illustrated* on February 18.

2003   The Cleveland Cavaliers sign James with their first draft pick.

2004   LeBron wins NBA Rookie of the Year; plays on the US Olympic basketball team; has a son, LeBron James Jr., with girlfriend, Savannah Brinson; starts LeBron James Family Foundation.

2006   The Cavaliers play in the NBA playoffs. They lose in the second round to the Detroit Pistons.

2007   The Cavaliers reach the NBA Finals but lose to the San Antonio Spurs. LeBron's second son, Bryce Maximus, is born.

2008   James plays on the US Olympic basketball team and wins a gold medal.

2010   James leaves the Cavaliers and joins the Miami Heat.

2011   The Heat reach the NBA Finals but lose to the Dallas Mavericks.

2012   The Heat win the NBA Finals. James is named NBA Finals MVP. He plays on the US Olympic basketball team and wins a gold medal.

2013   The Heat win the NBA Finals. LeBron marries Savannah Brinson.

2014   The Heat reach the NBA Finals but lose to the San Antonio Spurs. LeBron decides to return to the Cleveland Cavaliers. His daughter, Zhuri, is born.

2015   The Cavaliers reach the NBA Finals but lose to the Golden State Warriors. James stars in *Trainwreck*.

2016   The Cavaliers win the NBA Finals against the Golden State Warriors.

2017   The Cavaliers reach the NBA Finals but lose to the Golden State Warriors.

GLOSSARY

activism The act of speaking out or taking action to right a wrong.

amateur A person who takes part in something without getting paid.

Amateur Athletic Union (AAU) An amateur sports organization.

broadcast To show on television.

charity An institution or fund to aid the needy.

contract A legal agreement between two parties.

documentary A movie that tells a true-life story.

draft The process of choosing players to join a team.

forfeit To lose the right to play a game as punishment.

foundation A group supported by donations.

housing project A group of residential buildings partially funded by a government agency.

index finger The first finger on a hand, also called a pointer finger.

point guard The basketball player who directs the team's offense.

press conference A meeting where reporters interview one or more people.

professional A person who is paid to do something.

rookie A first-year player in a professional sport.

social injustice Unfairness against people or groups.

SUV A sport-utility vehicle.

sweep To win every game in a contest.

wide receiver A football player who plays offense and is usually the fastest on the team.

FOR MORE INFORMATION

Canada Basketball
1 Westside Drive
Etobicoke, ON M9C 1B2, Canada
(416) 614-8037
Website: http://www.basketball.ca/en
Canada Basketball is a nonprofit organization and the governing body for
basketball in Canada.

Cleveland Cavaliers
Quicken Loans Arena
One Center Court
Cleveland, OH 44115
Website: http://www.nba.com/cavaliers
Facebook: @cavs
(216) 420-2000
The Cleveland Cavaliers are a National Basketball Association team.

LeBron James Family Foundation
3800 Embassy Parkway
Suite 360
Akron, OH 44333
Website: http://lebronjamesfamilyfoundation.org
Facebook: @lebronjamesfamilyfoundation
The LeBron James Family Foundation aims to help children and young
adults, particularly in the Akron/Cleveland area in Ohio.

Naismith Memorial Basketball Hall of Fame
1000 Hall of Fame Avenue
Springfield, MA 01105
(877) 4HOOPLA

Website: http://www.hoophall.com
The Naismith Memorial Basketball Hall of Fame collects and displays
    everything having to do with basketball, players, and basketball history.

National Basketball League of Canada
75 Blackfriars Street
London, ON N6H 1K8, Canada
Website: http://www.nblcanada.ca
The National Basketball League of Canada is a Canadian professional
    men's basketball league.

FOR FURTHER READING

Bodden, Valerie. *LeBron James: Champion Basketball Star.* Minneapolis, MN: ABDO Publishing, 2014.

Bryant, Howard. *Legends: The Best Players, Games, and Teams in Basketball.* New York, NY: Puffin Books, 2017.

Ciovacco, Justine. *LeBron James: NBA Champion.* New York, NY: Rosen Publishing, 2016.

Gitlin, Marty. *LeBron James.* Minneapolis, MN: Sportszone, 2015.

Hill, Anne E. *LeBron James: King of Shots.* Minneapolis, MN: Twenty-First Century Books, 2013.

Indovino, Shaina. *LeBron James.* Broomall, PA: Mason Crest, 2015.

Leddy, Rick. *LeBron James: The King of the Game.* Beverly Hills, CA: Sole Books, 2015.

Morreale, Marie. *LeBron James.* New York, NY: Scholastic Inc., 2015.

Norwich, Grace. *I Am LeBron James: King of Shots.* New York, NY: Scholastic Inc., 2014.

Zuckerman, Gregory, with Elijah Zuckerman and Gabriel Zuckerman. *Rising Above: How 11 Athletes Overcame Challenges in Their Youth to Become Stars.* New York, NY: Puffin Books, 2017.

BIBLIOGRAPHY

Associated Press. "LeBron James' 61 points in win set career, Heat records." ESPN.com, March 4, 2014. http://www.espn.com/nba/recap?gameId=400489766.

Boren, Cindy, and Scott Allen. "'The people run this country': LeBron James doesn't regret calling Trump a 'bum.'" *Washington Post*, September 26, 2017. https://www.washingtonpost.com/news/early-lead/wp/2017/09/25/the-people-run-this-country-lebron-james-doesnt-regret-calling-trump-a-bum/?utm_term=.60dec2f773a0.

Chin, Mallory. "LeBron James Reminisces on His Journey to Becoming the Face of the NBA." Hypebeast.com, September 11, 2017. https://hypebeast.com/2017/9/lebron-james-strive-for-greatness-nike-lebron-15-2017-interview.

Gartland, Dan. "LeBron James is getting rave reviews for his acting in *Trainwreck*." *Sports Illustrated*, September 26, 2017. https://www.si.com/extra-mustard/2015/07/21/lebron-james-trainwreck-acting-comedy-reviews.

James, LeBron, as told to Lee Jenkins. "I'm Coming Home." *Sports Illustrated*, July 11, 2014. https://www.si.com/nba/2014/07/11/lebron-james-cleveland-cavaliers.

Jenkins, Lee. "Crowning the king: LeBron James is *Sports Illustrated*'s 2016 sportsperson of the year." *Sports Illustrated*, December 1, 2016. https://www.si.com/sportsperson/2016/12/01/lebron-james-sportsperson-of-the-year-sports-illustrated.

Lee, Michael. "NBA Finals 2012: James, Miami Heat rout Oklahoma Thunder to win championship." *Washington Post*, June 22, 2012. https://www.washingtonpost.com/sports/wizards/nba-finals-2012-lebron-james-miami-heat-rout-oklahoma-city-thunder-to-win-championship/2012/06/22/gJQAPLA7tV_story.html?utm_term=.934128043bd1.

McMenamin, Dave, and Brian Windhorst. "Champion Cavs drink it all in after lifting Cleveland's title drought." ABC News, via ESPN, June 20, 2016. http://abcnews.go.com/Sports/champion-cavs-drink-lifting -clevelands-title-drought/story?id=39994079.

Nagelhout, Ryan. *LeBron James: Basketball's King*. New York, NY: Lucent Press, 2017.

Rogers, Martin. "LeBron James focused on family not NBA Finals, after racist attack." *USA Today*, May 31, 2017. https://www.usatoday.com /story/sports/nba/2017/05/31/lebron-james-focused-family-not-nba -finals-after-racist-attack/102362612.

Wahl, Grant. "Ahead of His Class." *Sports Illustrated*, February 18, 2002. https://www.si.com/vault/2002/02/18/318739/ahead-of-his-class -ohio-high-school-junior-lebron-james-is-so-good-that-hes-already -being-mentioned-as-the-heir-to-air-jordan.

Windhorst, Brian, and Dave McMenamin. *Return of the King: LeBron James, the Cleveland Cavaliers, and the Greatest Comeback in NBA History*. New York, NY: Grand Central Publishing, 2017.

INDEX

ABOUT THE AUTHOR

Simone Payment has a degree in psychology from Cornell University and a master's degree in elementary education from Wheelock College. She is the author of numerous books for young adults. Another book from Rosen Publishing that she authored, *Navy SEALs: Special Operations for the U.S. Navy* (Inside Special Operations), won a Quick Picks for Reluctant Young Readers award from the American Library Association and is on the Nonfiction Honor List of Voice of Youth Advocates.

PHOTO CREDITS

Cover Elsa/Getty Images; pp. 4–5 Oleksii Sidorov/Shutterstock .com; p. 5 Getty Images; pp. 7, 16, 24, 30 (background) mark cinotti/Shutterstock.com; pp. 8–9 AF Archive/Alamy Stock Photo; pp. 11, 17 Sporting News Archive/Getty Images; p. 12 Wesley Hitt/ Getty Images; pp. 15, 22 © AP Images; p. 19 Hector Mata/AFP/ Getty Images; p. 20 Timothy A. Clary/AFP/Getty Images; p. 25 Larry Busacca/Getty Images; p. 26 Mark Ralston/AFP/Getty Images; p. 28 Alexander Tamargo/Getty Images; pp. 31, 36–37 Jason Miller/Getty Images; p. 33 Ronald Martinez/Getty Images.

Design: Michael Moy; Layout: Tahara Anderson;
Photo Researcher: Karen Huang